MONTSERRAT
EMERALD ISLE
OF THE CARIBBEAN

Howard A Fergus

Photographs
by
Hanna Dale

MACMILLAN CARIBBEAN

First published 1983

Published by
Macmillan Education
London and Basingstoke
*Companies and representatives in Lagos, Zaria, Manzini,
Gaborone, Nairobi, Singapore, Hong Kong, Delhi, Dublin,
Auckland, Melbourne, Tokyo, New York, Washington, Dallas.*

ISBN 0 333 35829 5

Printed in Hong Kong

Contents

Acknowledgements

We wish to record our thanks to Dr J A G Irish and the Old People's Welfare Association for permission to quote from their copyright publications; and to the Montserrat Tourist Board for allowing free use of its published literature.

All photographs by Hanna Dale except Nos. 1 and 15 which were taken by Michael Bourne and the two photographs of postage stamps which appear by courtesy of the Montserrat Philatelic Bureau.

Foreword

I welcome the production of this handbook on Montserrat. It is not the first, but it is the most comprehensive to be written. There is so little authentic information about the island that the mere arrival of this book is a remarkable event. Written by a local scholar who has contributed in several other ways to the development of the island, it makes interesting and insightful reading.

The book is of interest both to the Ministry which deals with Tourism as well as to my own Ministry. It is an indispensable visitors' companion and a valuable reference for all categories of persons who serve the tourist industry. In addition, its varied topics and photographs make it a useful resource text for social studies in schools. Finally, the book introduces Montserratians to important aspects of their history and culture.

This book deserves a wide audience and it is with pleasure that I recommend it.

Franklin A L Margetson,
Minister of Education, Health,
and Community Services

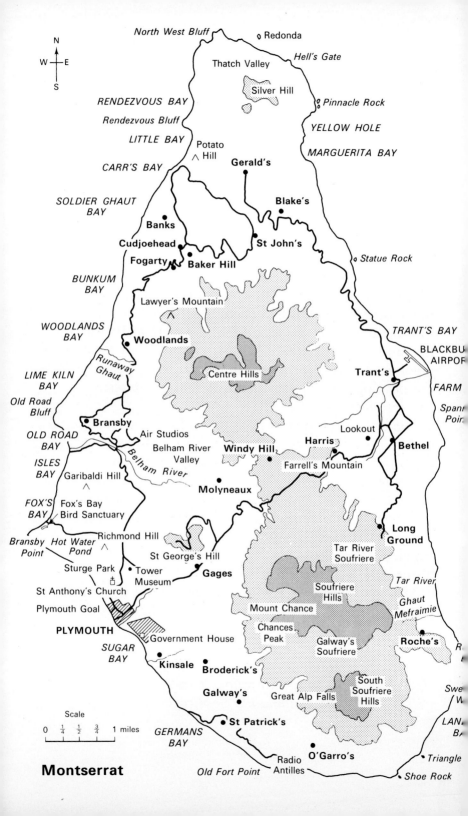

Montserrat

Introduction

Montserrat, a Caribbean tropic haven, has a unique character, the hallmark of which is natural beauty, quiet pleasures and friendly people. This book unveils the special Montserrat package. That it is written with visitors in mind is evident. Nearly half of the text deals with what there is to see and do, and with the kind of information that the visitor requires. The book is not, however, a conventional tourist guide. Indeed, certain specific information, such as hotel rates, is lacking.

This is really a handbook — a general introduction to the island — as well as a souvenir of its memorable places, its beauty and its culture. It is wide-ranging in content: plant life, animal life, history, geography, government and folk culture. It thus offers insights for those who wish to read more about the island, or even to research various aspects of its life. It should, therefore, be useful as a student's companion. For those visitors who wish to know more about the island than where to dine and play golf, and how big a tip to give, this amplified guide should be welcome.

If there is any credit for the book, the bulk should go to the photographer, Hanna Dale. It was her idea; it was her enthusiasm that triggered my pen. It is, perhaps, significant that this particular introduction to the island is being made jointly by a temporary resident and a born and bred islander.

From this joint perspective, meet Montserrat.

Howard A Fergus

CHAPTER ONE
Physical Setting

Corrugated hillsides
Leaping in giddy jumps
Towards the cloud-specked sky.

(Norman Buffonge, Montserratian Poet)

Topography

Montserrat, a pear-shaped island, lies between 16°40' and 16°50' north latitude and between 62°9' and 62°15' west longitude in the Leeward group of the Lesser Antilles. It is about 11 miles (18 km) long and 7 miles (11 km) wide with an area of 39½ square miles (102 sq km). Antigua, 27 miles (43 km) to the northeast and Guadeloupe, about the same distance to the southeast, are its closest neighbours. Several ravines, or ghauts as they are locally called, notch the lower slopes of the island's many hills and mountains.

Three lofty, green-clad mountain ranges flaunt the skyline. The northern range, the Silver Hills, ends in a bold headland; the southern range descends in a cliff to the sea, which abounds in break-away boulders. The tallest range, the Soufriere Hills, rises to 3,002 feet above sea level at Mount Chance, whose summit is almost always obscured by clouds.

The island is volcanic in origin and the Soufriere

1

A view of Chance's Peak looking across the Belham Valley (Michael Bourne)

group of hills houses the craters of extinct volcanoes and active fumaroles. The Galway's crater, south of Plymouth, is an awesome and arresting sight. J Davy, an early English traveller, described it as 'horror in the lap of beauty'. From boiling and shifting vents, it gives off sulphurous vapours and chemical deposits. Some of the hot springs from the Soufriere find their way to the valleys to form bathing lakes to which curative powers are attributed. The best known is the Hot Water Pond, just outside Plymouth. Its waters allegedly will cure rheumatism and other diseases, but only after a coin is thrown in as an offering to its guardian spirit.

The soils are volcanic and generally rock-strewn. Fertility varies from area to area, and erosion is a constant problem because of the steep slopes and careless agricultural practices.

Natural vegetation is confined mostly to the summits of the Soufriere and Centre Hills, where elfin

2

A view from Isles Bay on to the Golf Course and Vue Pointe with Redonda and Nevis on the horizon

woodlands of mosses, lichens and orchids occur. Around South Soufriere and Silver Hills, 'acacia savannahs' are common, as are cacti and sage bush.

At the foot of the hills, on gentle slopes, lie villages and farm lands. The villages are linked to each other and to the town on the western side of the island by well-paved roads. Sheltered bays are few, but Plymouth is served by a semi-deep water harbour.

Climate

Montserrat has a healthy tropical and maritime climate. Average temperatures range from 81 to 82 degrees Fahrenheit from July to October and 76 to 77 degrees in January. Northeast sea breezes fan the island for most of the year. The rainfall is about 60 inches annually, but the distribution is uneven throughout the island and throughout the year. The rainy season is normally from November to February and the dry season from March to June, but showers may be expected during the hurricane season, from July to October. December, January and February tend to be cool months.

Because of its bracing climate, Montserrat used to be referred to as 'The Montpellier of the West'. The climate supports a luxuriant vegetation with emerald hills and ravines of feathery ferns. Cultivated gardens, decking island homes, complement the scenic beauty.

CHAPTER TWO
Island History

On November 11, 1493, Admiral Columbus named a tiny island in the Leewards arc 'Santa Maria de Monserrate'. The sierras of the island reminded him of the mountainous location of the abbey of Montserrat near Barcelona in Spain. That monastery is famous as the place where Ignatius Loyola experienced a vision which led to his formation of the order of the Jesuits. If we are to believe Columbus and his Indian girl guides, the Caribs had killed off the Arawak population and left the island without inhabitants. In any case, Columbus was too busy with visions and delusions of gold and Cipangu (Japan) to explore the island's rugged hills or even to land on its grey and ebony sands. By the middle of the seventeenth century, the Caribs no longer lived on the island, although they raided thereafter from time to time.

Very little is known of the pre-history of Montserrat. Archeological sites have been identified at Trant's and at the Belham River Valley Golf Course, and Amerindian artefacts have been found in topsoil at various other places. Most of the finds are small images, household goods and mascots, representing human faces. They resemble similar works of art from Mexico and Central America. One particular artefact, a 'modelled adorno', which can be dated

The ruins at Trant's Estate

between 500 BC and 500 AD, points to the possibility of pre-Arawak life on Montserrat. We know that the Caribs named the island Alliouagana (land of the prickly bush). A fertile field of archeological investigation still exists.

The Spaniards did not settle Montserrat. The honour was reserved for Thomas Warner, who arrived there with a British contingent from the mother colony of St Kitts — a Leeward Islands' version of the English Pilgrim Fathers. The colonists were English and Irish Catholics, who were made uncomfortable in Protestant St Kitts. In Montserrat, they found a new shrine for their faith and a haven from Protestant persecution. News of a Roman Catholic asylum in this corner of the Antilles soon spread across the Atlantic to the British North American colony of Virginia; in 1633, Catholic refugees, pushed out of Virginia by Episcopalian persecution, also came hither in search of unmolested altars. Montserrat was thus unique in being established as an Irish-Catholic Caribbean colony. When, in 1649, following his victory at Drogheda (in Ireland), Cromwell sent some of his political prisoners to Montserrat, he both increased the population and preserved its Irish character.*

Sugar and Slaves

Montserrat developed into a typical sugar and slave colony in the seventeenth century. At first largely a tobacco island, it started growing small quantities of sugar by 1649. Slavery was the handmaid of the sugar industry in the Caribbean, thus the date of the arrival of the first slaves would correspond roughly with the start of sugar culture. The first slaves arrived by 1651, at the latest. In that year, Irishman John Blake, of the English Guinea Company, called in at Montserrat with a number of slaves. Slaves quickly outnumbered the original British indentured servants, but not to the same extent as they did in Barbados and St Kitts.

With sugar-and-slaves, over-mighty planters began to emerge. Samuel Waad was typical of these. When Governor Roger Osborne sentenced him to be shot in 1654, and confiscated his property, it consisted of 70 head of cattle, 500 sheep, 2 horses, 2 colts, many pigs, 30 Christian servants and 50 slaves.

By 1655, the characteristic colonial social structure was evident: an Anglo-Irish planter class, a number of *Christian* servants and an ever increasing population of black slaves. In 1671, there were 523 slaves. By 1678, the number of slaves had risen to 992 or 26% of the total population. The slave population grew until blacks had outnumbered whites.

A sprinkling of whites in a large sea of blacks gave rise to fear, repression and rebellion. The whites,

*Chapter Three is devoted to Montserrat's Irish connections.

Table 1 — Census of 1678

	Men	Women	Children	Total
English	346	175	240	761
Irish	769	410	690	1869
Scottish	33	6	13	52
Whites	1148	591	943	2682
Blacks	400	300	292	992

fearing a black rebellion, passed repressive laws to control and coerce the blacks. The blacks, on the other hand, resented oppression, and consequently rebelled. The March 17, 1768 rebellion is the best documented. St Patrick's Day was aptly chosen since the Irish planter lords would be steeped in commemoration. The plan was for the slaves within Government House to seize the swords of the gentlemen, the remaining fighters firing into the house with such missiles as they could muster. But the plans were overheard by a woman who leaked it to the masters, and the slaves, mulattoes and free blacks involved were all cruelly executed. The rebels of 1768 are today regarded as freedom fighters, and the anniversary of their attempted coup is celebrated.

Anglo-French Rivalry

In the seventeenth and eighteenth centuries, Caribbean waters became the thoroughfare of French and English soldiers as these nations competed for mastery in the sugar islands. Montserrat felt the depredations of the wars. It was invaded several times by the French, and they captured and held it twice. It was captured during the second Dutch War,

1665-1667, but returned at the *Treaty of Breda*. The French were helped by the Irish, who were suffering from religious discrimination. General De Barre crushed the English, but left 500 Irish and their possessions intact. The Montserratian Irish again helped the French in the sortie of 1717. Montserrat was taken in 1781 during the Caribbean phase of the wars associated with the American revolt (1776-83) and was actually French for about nine months. At the *Treaty of Versailles* (1783) following Rodney's brilliant battle at Les Saintes, Montserrat returned to the English fold and has stayed ever since.

Changing Fortunes

Fortunes were made by the few through the oppression of the many as the island was carved up into *latifundia* or large estates. John Blake of Ireland and Queely Sheill were among the men who made

A traditional bread oven which is still in use today

fortunes in Montserrat. One owned property in the north and the other in the south of the island. Sugar production peaked in 1735, when 3,150 tons were produced. Planter and historian Bryan Edwards tells that, in 1791, production in Montserrat was as follows: 'In sugar, six thousand acres; in cotton, provisions and pasturage, two thousand each. None other of the other tropical staples are produced or raised. Its average crop from 1784 to 1788 was 2,737 hogsheads of sugar of sixteen hundred weight, 1,107 puncheons of rum, and 275 bales of cotton.'

Sugar fortunes started to wane towards the end of the eighteenth century. Earthquakes, drought, hurricanes, French raids, absentee land owners and short-sighted farming methods all took their toll. The loss of slave labour after emancipation in 1834 finally undermined the foundation of the traditional planter class.

In the middle of the nineteenth century, many properties became encumbered with debt and were sold out. Estates were cultivated by *metayage* or share-cropping and black labourers occupied cottages and grew food crops on estate lands as tenants-at-will. Quaker Joseph Sturge, of anti-slavery fame, was among those who bought estates on the island. In 1869, the Sturge's Montserrat Company was formed under the directorship of his son. By 1916, the Company (renamed Montserrat Company Limited) owned nearly half the island with estates at Olveston, Woodlands, the Grove, Richmond, Fryes, Isles Bay, O'Garro's, Brades, Tar River, Elberton and Fogarty's. Sturge Park, the recreation ground in Plymouth, was donated by the Montserrat Company and so named to perpetuate the memory of the founder of their fortunes.

When sugar collapsed, limes and cotton replaced it. Limes, introduced by Francis Burke and financed by

Edmund Sturge in 1852, was a good Quaker crop. Lime juice as an alternative to alcohol appealed to the teetotal temper of the Quakers. (A condition attached to the grant of Sturge Park was that no alcohol was to be sold there — a condition now more honoured in the breach than the observance.) Limes prospered and Montserrat lime juice became famous in New Zealand, Australia and Britain. Montserrat lime juice was particularly in demand in the British navy for tanning and for drinking. It was drunk to check scurvy among the sailors. It is said to have given the abrasive nickname 'Limey' to the British.

After a hurricane destroyed many of the lime orchards in 1899, the island turned to cotton. Cotton reached its zenith in 1941, when 5,395 acres produced 1,175,932 pounds of lint. The economy of the island continued to be based on cotton until the nineteen sixties.

Modern Times

By the middle of the twentieth century, export agriculture was in decline. Montserratians emigrated

A cotton field

in droves. After emancipation, the freedmen went to Trinidad and British Guiana, where wages were high; at the turn of the twentieth century, with sugar and limes failing, they went to Panama and the United States; later the pull was to Cuba, Santo Domingo (1911-1921) and to the oil refineries of Curaçao and Aruba. The mass exodus to the United Kingdom in the nineteen fifties and sixties was, therefore, only the most recent wave in a continual current of migration. Over 5,000 persons emigrated to the United Kingdom between 1946 and 1964. It was both cause and effect of the decline of the cotton industry.

During this period, trade unionism developed; universal adult suffrage gave the poor man the vote; by 1952, working-class leaders had replaced the merchant-planter oligarchy, which had succeeded the pre-emancipation plantocratic regime. Robert W Griffith was the first trade union leader (1946), but he was soon superseded by W H Bramble, who combined both trade union leadership and political office and became the island's first Chief Minister in 1961. It was left to these leaders to rebuild the island's economy in the last half of the century.

Remittances from emigrants to the United Kingdom and elsewhere made a big impression on the economy, but when the flood of postal and money orders became a trickle, it was to real estate-and-home-construction that the island turned. From around 1960, marginal estate lands, and some not so marginal, were carved up for expatriate home sites. North Americans and Britons built many a Roman-type *country* villa for winter hideouts, and Montserrat's *resident* tourists were born. Real estate development brought more of the regular tourists, as the island's infrastructure and general living standards improved. Montserrat's struggle towards modernisation is evident in its search for

12

industrial enterprises. Tax holidays and other inducements have brought a number of industries, mostly of the assembling type.

The economy of the island is buoyant; housing and health are comparatively good; in 1981, the island felt no need for British budgetary aid. The fact that an agricultural revival continues to elude government gives cause for concern, especially in view of Montserrat's massive food import bill. Fortunately, perhaps, the island has had a negative population growth since 1946. This is one reason why it experiences no real poverty.

CHAPTER THREE
The Irish Legacy

In recent times, many peoples have been showing interest in their 'roots'. Many Irishmen, investigating the Caribbean route of the Irish diaspora, have made Montserrat the object of special study.

Among the Irish retentions which anthropologist, John Messenger, claims to exist, are linguistic patterns, systems of values, codes of etiquette, musical styles, smuggling and an Irish recipe for stew. It is not easy to separate what is distinctly Irish or African in many aspects of the culture. In most cases, cultural retentions are Afro-Irish combines, with a 'New World' interpretation.

Irish influence is obvious in certain national emblems. A carved Irish shamrock still adorns the gable at Government House. (According to tradition, Irish St Patrick used the shamrock to illustrate the doctrine of the Trinity.) The island's flag and crest show a lady with a cross and a harp. The lady is Erin of Irish legend, who gave Ireland its second name. An early writer on Montserrat referred to it as Erin:

> The slow years passed, and Cromwell's Irish
> came
> And found another Erin in your soil.

Between 1903 and 1951, and as recently as 1982, the lady with the harp was printed on Montserrat stamps.

A view from the Tarr River Estate on to Roche's Bluff

An Irish heritage is evident in the names of the places and the people of the island. Montserrat is said to have been called 'The Emerald Isle of the West', because of its green beauty and its Irish names, such as Farrell's, St Patrick's, Rileys, Fogarty, Fergus Mountain, Blakes, Galway's, Reid's Hill, Banks, Kinsale, Cork Hill, Sweeney's, O'Garro's. These are the names of estates, villages, heights and shorelines. Planters gave names to their estates and their slaves; therefore some of these place names are now the names of persons. Common Christian names in Montserrat include: Irish, Farrell, O'Brien, Riley, Fergus, O'Garro, Galloway, Ryan and Roach.

It is widely claimed that Montserratians speak with a 'distinct brogue' and a 'lilt' which are attributed to the Irish connection. This nineteenth century story, though probably fictitious, illustrates the claim.

> *Montserrat had Irish colonists for its early settlers and the negroes to this day have the Connaught brogue curiously engrafted on the African jargon. It is said that a Connaught man on arriving at Montserrat, was, to his astonishment, hailed in vernacular*

Irish by a negro from one of the first boats that came alongside. 'Thunder and turf,' exclaimed Pat, 'how long have you been here?' 'Three months! And so black already! Hanum a diaul,' says Pat, thinking Quashie a country man, 'I'll not stay among ye;' and in a few hours the Connaught man was on his return, with a white skin to the Emerald Isle.

The habits of ending sentences with the emphatic phrase 'at all' or 'at all at all' and the substitution of other responders for yes and no, such as 'uhm-h'm' and 'e-eehn', are regarded as Irish.

Although Montserrat was settled mostly by Irish Catholics, the official church was the Church of England. This was because it was an English colony ruled firmly by England and it would have been against the ecclesiastical policy of the time to make a Roman Catholic church the official one. In fact, Catholic persecution in Britain had its parallel in Anglo-Irish Montserrat. In the seventeenth century, Catholic priests had to be smuggled in disguised as fishermen or, as in the case of Father John Stritch, as a merchant and wood buyer. Persecution did not stamp out Catholicism, and in St Patrick's, which was the area of greatest Irish concentration, it is still the dominant religion.

The Irish seem to have left their mark on music. One of the drums played in orchestras, and the method of playing, are probably influenced by the Irish drum called a bodhran. A popular local dance to a folk song, *Bam-chick-lay Chiga Foot Maya*, strongly resembles certain Irish step-dances.

'Goat water', the national dish, is an Irish-type stew made with kiddy meat. Some claim that it was introduced by Irish settlers, while others argue that a

Cooking goat water

similar recipe for goat meat exists in parts of Africa. Anthropologist John Messenger has no doubt that 'goat water' is Irish in origin because, in 1965, an aged Connemara housewife gave his wife a recipe identical to the delicious Montserrat pottage.

Racial and religious persecution was prevalent in Montserrat. National feelings and cleavages ran high among Montserrat's Britons and, in 1668, Governor Stapleton had to legislate against abrasive and abusive name-calling. He passed a law 'to restrain several odious distinctions used by the English, Scots and Irish reflecting on each other (English Dog, Scots Dog, Cavalier, Roundhead and many other approbrious, scandalous and disgraceful terms)'.

Undoubtedly, Montserrat still has a touch of Ireland, even if it is not always clear what is decidedly Irish, English, Scottish, or even African. There is still room for research. The Irish, for much of their sojourn, were treated as second class citizens and even rebels. Thus, they left but few distinct, indelible marks on the Montserrat society.

CHAPTER FOUR
Government, People and Products

Government

In 1971, a writer remarked that Montserrat was likely to be Britain's last colony. Montserrat continues to be unrepentant over its colonial status, and there are no signs that it will ask for independence in the immediate future. The official position is that economic independence must precede political independence, if the latter is to be much more than a new constitution,

Government House

a new flag and a new anthem; although no one has really defined economic independence. When, in 1967, her eastern Caribbean neighbours became states-in-association with Britain, Montserrat chose to retain colony status as in the beginning when Charles I included it in the proprietary patent of the spendthrift Earl of Carlisle.

A British dependent territory, Montserrat has a representative government with a ministerial system. It practises parliamentary democracy rooted in the Westminster model. The British monarch, who is Head of State, is represented by a Governor; and appeals can be made from local and regional courts to His or Her Majesty's Privy Council. Britain is responsible for the island's external affairs, defence and law and order, generally. In the British 1981 Nationality Act, Montserratians are designated Citizens of the British Dependent Territories.

The Government consists of a Legislative Council and an Executive Council. Elections are held every five years for the Legislative Council and the party gaining the majority of seats in the seven constituency legislature forms the Government. The head of government is styled Chief Minister, and there are three other Ministers responsible respectively for: Education, Health and Community Affairs; Agriculture, Trade, Lands and Housing; Communications and Works. A Financial Secretary, an Attorney General, and two Nominated Members complete the eleven-member chamber which is presided over by a Speaker. This is the island's law-making body.

The formalities and procedures adopted in the legislature closely resemble those of its parent British Parliament. A mace, the Speaker's symbol of authority, is carried before him as is done at Westminster. Sittings of the House are open to the public although, as in Britain, they are termed 'strangers'.

Executive Council is similar to a Cabinet. It comprises the four Ministers of Government, the Financial Secretary and the Attorney General, who is the Crown's Principal Law Officer. The Governor presides over Executive Council in closed deliberations. This Chamber makes policies and the day-to-day administrative decisions. It meets weekly, in contrast to the Legislative Council, which meets in an *ad hoc* manner.

In addition to the usual ceremonial functions, the Governor of Montserrat exercises executive authority. As head of the civil service, he is responsible for its management and efficiency. He is responsible for defence, internal security and external affairs and has some of the duties of a Minister of Home Affairs. In certain judicial cases, he exercises the sovereign's prerogative of mercy, although in this, and in other areas of his reserve powers, he tends to act after he has been advised by the Executive Council.

Regional Co-operation

Attempts to unify groups of British territories politically in the Caribbean have a long history. The aim of the British has been to reduce the cost of colonial administration. Montserrat was involved in one such attempt as early as 1668, but inter-island jealousies and squabbles brought about its early death. In 1871, Montserrat, Antigua, St Kitts and the British Virgin Islands (for a period including Dominica), were formed into a federation of the Leeward Islands. This loose union shared only a Governor, a police force, audit and a few other subjects. It finally dissolved to enable each territory to enter the larger West Indies Federation of 1958 as separate units. That grand attempt at political federation collapsed in 1961, but various forms of functional co-operation exist among the territories. There is co-operation in education, shipping and, to some extent, currency, but the greatest emphasis is on economic matters.

Montserrat is a member of the regional trading and economic partnership known as the Caribbean Economic Community (CARICOM). The other members are Antigua and Barbuda, Barbados, Belize, Dominica, Jamaica, Grenada, St Kitts, St Lucia, St Vincent, Guyana and Trinidad and Tobago. CARICOM grew out of the Caribbean Free Trade Association (CARIFTA) formed in 1968. Montserrat also belongs to the sub-regional Organisation of East Caribbean States (OECS) which co-operates in political as well as socio-economic affairs.

Friendships

Montserrat's foreign relations are controlled by the British Government. Its colonial relations, trading ties, and its general geo-political setting, predispose it towards friendship with the United States and Canada. Friendly relations have also been established with West Germany and Venezuela. The present Government has expressed deep faith in free enterprise and friendship with the United States. Prospective governments may be less euphoric over this friendship, but even in independence, a pro-United States and pro-Western relationship is likely to prevail in the island. Cultural and social ties with the United States are very deep-rooted.

The People

Preliminary figures from the 1980 census put the population of Montserrat at about 12,000. Throughout the twentieth century, the figure has remained stable due to emigration and, more recently, to birth

Young Montserratians at sunset on Sugar Bay

control measures. Most of the people are black, but there is a sprinkling of brown and the odd white. More recently, an infusion of white North American and European residents has somewhat altered the colour profile.

The official language is English, but a dialect is widely spoken on informal occasions. Here is an example of the local patois: *If awee me come li quicka, yuh woulda get an me woulda get...* This may be translated: If we had arrived a little sooner, both of us would have got... Or: *A ya me born; a ya me rear*; meaning; I was born and raised here.

Anglican, Methodist and Roman Catholic are the main religious denominations, but the Seventh Day Adventist and Evangelical persuasions are assuming an increasing importance. Sects, like Jehovah's Witness and Bahai, exist in small pockets.

The friendliness of its people is one of the island's proud assets.

Economy

The economy, based mainly on agriculture, real estate, building construction, tourism and assembling industries, has little manufacturing activity. It is, therefore, heavily dependent on the importation of capital and consumer goods. Despite its decline, agriculture is still one of the main occupations, although much of it is subsistence farming. The Government has plans to revive farming to the point where the youth are attracted to it. A variety of vegetables and fruits such as cabbages, sweet potatoes, carrots, onions, lettuce, christophenes, pumpkins, bananas, avocado pears, sugar apples, mammie apples, mangoes, guavas, soursops, melons, paw paws, pineapples and passion fruit are grown for domestic use and for export.

The building trade is a big employer. A continually expanding tourist trade earns much needed foreign exchange and provides a variety of jobs. The Government, however, plans to avoid high-rise hotels and noisy night clubs and to highlight instead a quieter, gentler life with simple pleasures. A true escape from the hectic life of the developed north as well as from the headier pace of the developing south can be found in Montserrat. The avowed aim here is to maintain it as a model of 'the way the Caribbean used to be'.

Industrial activity is on the increase but mostly consists of assembly work in electronics and textiles. The finished products are generally sent back to parent companies (outside CARICOM) for marketing.

The island is beginning to build an integrated cotton industry. Fortunately, the quantity of cotton now grown is adequate for this purpose. The excellent quality sea island cotton, sought after by Japan and certain countries of the industrial north, is being pro-

The Saturday market in Plymouth

cessed at home into yarn, and made in turn into articles for sale. The click-clack of looms and the sound of machines constitute a noisy landmark. In the heyday of cotton Montserrat, purely a primary producer, kept the mills of Lancashire turning. Any boasting, however, has to be muffled. If the cotton acreage increases, it will still be more profitable to export some than to process all at home. This is because the island lacks the technology to handle large volumes of cotton. Countries like Japan would be able to process such volumes at much lower cost.

Important by-products such as cooking oil and animal feed will come from the cotton. There is really nothing new about these two vital products, since the Montserrat Company once manufactured them for decades. In local parlance, they were called 'sweet oil' and 'cotton cake'.

A developing country, with few natural resources,

the island tends to embrace novel opportunities for augmenting the public purse. An off-shore medical school and off-shore banking fall in this category. Students from the United States mainly, and a few from African and Asian countries, study pre-clinical medicine on the island. This is another version of an enclave industry. It is a commercial enterprise, licensed like a company and owned by a businessman/educator. The parent company is in the United States of America. To stretch the commercial analogy, it is something of a 'multi-national' venture.

Off-shore banks are mostly of the 'paper' type existing in a plaque at a lawyer's office and in a couple of legal documents. They are sometimes set up to conduct one transaction. It is Americans who usually traffic in these banks which make the United States Government ill at ease. Off-shore banks are often perceived as a means of dodging taxes and engaging in other dubious financial dealings. The Montserrat Government has painstakingly passed laws to ensure that the banks which operate within the country are reputable.

CHAPTER FIVE
Welcome to Montserrat

Getting There

The maxim of a leading Montserrat hotel is 'our house is your house', and this seems to be the message of Montserratian hospitality. Although a sequestered retreat, Montserrat is easily accessible. It is 15 flying minutes away from Antigua's International Coolidge Airport. Coolidge is 3 hours jet time from Miami, $3\frac{1}{2}$ hours from New York, $4\frac{1}{2}$ hours from Toronto and $8\frac{1}{2}$ hours from London. A network of air routes links the Caribbean region with Montserrat via Antigua. Apart from the convenient connections from Montserrat by Montserrat Air Services and Leeward Islands Air Transport (LIAT), charters are readily available. The jetstrip of Guadeloupe is only minutes away from Montserrat and therefore provides another gateway.

Entry Formalities

Citizens of the United Kingdom, the United States of America and Canada must have a valid return ticket and present a valid identification document, which could be either a passport, a driver's license, a birth certificate or a registration card. Other visitors need to have a valid passport and an onward or return

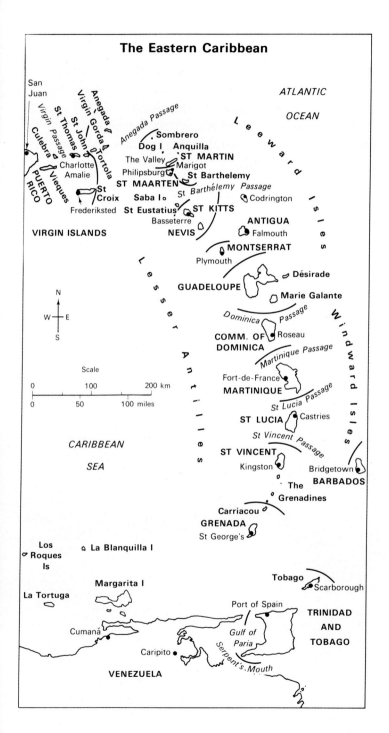

The Eastern Caribbean

ATLANTIC

OCEAN

San Juan

Virgin Passage

Virgin Gorda

Anegada

St Thomas

St John

Tortola

Culebra

Vieques

PUERTO RICO

Charlotte Amalie

St Croix

Frederiksted

VIRGIN ISLANDS

Anegada Passage

Sombrero

Dog I. Anquilla

The Valley

ST MARTIN

Marigot

Philipsburg

St Barthelemy

ST MAARTEN

St Barthélemy Passage

Saba I.

St Eustatius

ST KITTS

Basseterre

NEVIS

Codrington

ANTIGUA

Falmouth

MONTSERRAT

Plymouth

GUADELOUPE

Désirade

Marie Galante

Dominica Passage

COMM. OF DOMINICA

Roseau

Martinique Passage

Fort-de-France

MARTINIQUE

St Lucia Passage

ST LUCIA

Castries

St Vincent Passage

ST VINCENT

Kingston

The Grenadines

Bridgetown

BARBADOS

Carriacou

GRENADA

St George's

Leeward Isles

Windward Isles

Lesser Antilles

N
W — E
S

Scale

0   100   200 km

0   50   100 miles

CARIBBEAN

SEA

Los Roques Is

La Blanquilla I

Margarita I

Tobago

Scarborough

La Tortuga

Port of Spain

TRINIDAD AND TOBAGO

Cumaná

Gulf of Paria

Caripito

Serpent's Mouth

VENEZUELA

ticket. Without such a ticket, visitors may be required on arrival to deposit an adequate sum to cover repatriation. All visitors should be able to satisfy the immigration authorities that they can keep themselves financially while on the island.

Persons from countries where smallpox, yellow fever, cholera and similar contagious diseases are reported, should have a valid vaccination certificate.

Visitors are allowed to take in 200 cigarettes or 50 cigars, 6 fluid ounces of perfume, wines and spirits not exceeding 40 fluid ounces and a reasonable quantity of personal effects without paying duty. Gift articles costing up to EC$250.00 are allowed, provided that the visitor was not on the island during the previous twelve months.

Pets may be imported under certain conditions, but the advice of the Veterinary Officer, c/o Agricultural Department, The Groves, Montserrat, should be obtained.

Sunset

Accommodation

Given the island's size, it has a comfortable range of accommodation. There are in-town inns and country hideaways; luxury resorts and homelier hotels. Guest houses, apartments, condominiums and private villas (many with swimming pools) complete the accommodation shopping list. Some peep from promontory and hilltop, some look up to towering mountains from the hum of the town, and others command a panorama of sea, mountain and verdant 'river' valley. Most reinforce the feeling and reality of tranquillity, which is an enviable hallmark of this tropic isle.

Leading hotels
Vue Pointe (Tel. 5210/5211);
Caribelle (Tel. 2641);
Hideaway (Tel. 5252);
Springs (Tel. 2481/2482);
Coconut Hill (Tel. 2144);
Wade Inn (Tel. 2881).

Main apartments
Shamrock Condominiums (Tel. 2434) and Lime Court Apartments (Tel. 2513), both of which are in Plymouth.

Main villa representatives
Neville Bradshaw Agencies Ltd, PO Box 250, Plymouth, Montserrat, West Indies (Tel. 5270);

D R V (Frank) Edwards, Montserrat Estates, PO Box 58, Plymouth, Montserrat, West Indies (Tel. 2431);

Jacquie Ryan Real Estate, PO Box 425, Plymouth, Montserrat, West Indies (Tel. 2055).

If you choose a self-catering facility, the supermarkets can supply you with a variety of imported foods and with some local vegetables. The Plymouth outdoor market supplies fruits and fresh vegetables according to the season. The market comes to life on Fridays and Saturdays especially, and is a lively and colourful scene where speech, dress, higgling and selling customs give a graphic commentary on the indigenous culture. Plans are afoot to increase the quantity of local fruits and vegetables. The island plans to feed itself and link tourism to agriculture.

Maid service is generally provided with self-catering facilities; baby sitters can be arranged for. The word 'domestic assistant' or 'domestic help' is gradually being preferred to 'maid'. The latter tends to connote a semi-servile person who was used by the wealthy a generation ago and who was distinguished by a special livery consisting of a white cap and white bib.

Accommodation may be booked with property management offices or through the Montserrat Tourist Board, which keeps an updated list. Montserrat's tourism representatives in Miami and Toronto, and the Eastern Caribbean Tourist Association offices in New York and London, can supply information on accommodation.

Presently, there is a 7% Government accommodation tax and a 10% service charge on accommodation bills. An airport services tax of U S $5.00 (EC$5.00 for citizens of CARICOM) is payable on departure at Blackburne.

Getting Around

Its sleepy lanes and woodlands paths make Montserrat a good place for walking. Auto transport is, however, necessary. A number of companies and individuals offer self-drive car rentals. Cars are mostly of Japanese manufacture. Cars with automatic gear transmissions, or with standard shift, are available. The visitor can secure a temporary license at the airport or at the police traffic office in Plymouth, but he needs to present a valid driving licence. Driving, incidentally, is on the left hand side of the road. The roads in Montserrat are, perhaps, the best in the Eastern Caribbean, despite the island's hilly terrain.

Taxis are numerous and are available for specific journeys or for sightseeing excursions. Fares are officially fixed from point to point, as are mileages for island tours. Many taxi drivers have attended courses mounted by the Tourist Board in conjunction with the University of the West Indies Extra-Mural Centre, and are therefore qualified to serve visitors. Some are quite knowledgeable on titbits of local history. Out-of-town hotels generally provide daily transportation to Plymouth for hotel guests; mini buses run regularly between Plymouth and outlying villages.

Montserratians prefer not to be 'progressive' in certain areas of dress. Nude or topless bathing and living 'in the natural', have not taken on; swim-wear is not acceptable for wearing in Plymouth in bars, restaurants, banks, stores or Government offices.

On the other hand, formal suits for men are the exception rather than the rule. Personal taste and culture may dictate here, but shirt jacs and sport shirts are suitable for men, and make sense in the climate. Light cotton dresses, slacks, and shorts are suitable for women all year round. A wrap or light cardigan is useful for the cool evenings of December, January and February, and perhaps a long skirt.

Light canvas shoes are preferable to sandals for walks and nature trails.

Miscellaneous Information

The main public holidays are New Year's Day, Good Friday, Easter Monday, Labour Day (first Monday in

A selection of Montserrat's attractive postage stamps (Montserrat Philatelic Bureau)

May), Whit Monday (seventh Monday after Easter Monday), August Monday (first Monday in August), Liberation/Discovery Day (November 11), Christmas Day and Boxing Day (December 26). St Patrick's Day (March 17) was added to the list in 1983.

Shops and business houses are generally open from 8.00 am to 12.00 noon and from 1.00 pm to 4.00 pm daily, except Wednesdays and Saturdays, when the hours are 8.00 am to 1.00 pm, with a few supermarkets opening until 3.00 pm.

Montserrat sells colourful and informative stamps. Collectors can obtain these through the Montserrat Philatelic Bureau, as well as from the Post Office.

Telecommunication services

Cable and Wireless Limited operates an island-wide telephone system and telex, cable and telephone on international lines. Montserrat is four hours behind Greenwich Mean Time and one hour ahead of Eastern Standard Time.

The Government Radio Station, Radio Montserrat (ZJB) and Radio Antilles, provide daily broadcasting services including international, regional, and local news, current affairs and musical programmes. ZJB operates on the medium wave band at 885 Khz, and Radio Antilles at 930 Khz in English and 740 Khz in French. The island is within range of a large number of regional and international broadcasting stations.

Antilles Television, a local television station, relays Antigua and Barbuda (ABS-TV) on Channel 7. Locally produced programmes, especially featuring news, sports and culture, are televised. Current discussions reveal that it will not be long before cable and satellite television invade the emerald isle.

Currency and banking

The Eastern Caribbean dollar is the official currency, but the American dollar is widely used. The exchange rate is around EC$2.66 per US$1.00. There is a Government tax of 1% on the 'sales' of foreign currency.

The Royal Bank of Canada and Barclays are the main banks, but there is a Government Savings Bank housed in the Treasury Buildings, and the Montserrat Building Society, which traffics in mortgage financing for homes, also operates as a bank. In addition, an American 'commercial' bank conducts a limited range of local transactions. The Royal Bank of Canada is the oldest bank in Montserrat, having started operations in 1917.

Electricity

The electric current is 220 volts, 60 cycles, but many modern houses also carry 110 volts. Electrical outlets tend to take mostly three-pronged plugs.

Medical Services

These are reasonably adequate on the island — a far cry from the days when two doctors served the entire populace. A number of private medical practitioners are available and doctors in the Government health service also practise privately. Glendon Hospital in Plymouth provides surgical, medical, obstetric, paediatric and dental services, and has sixty-eight beds. Because of the size of the island and its hospital services, cases requiring specialist treatment are sent to the University of the West Indies hospital in Jamaica or elsewhere in the region. Provision is made for the periodic visit of eye surgeons, opticians and ear specialists.

There have not been any serious epidemics in recent years and no malarial mosquitoes exist. A number of health centres are scattered throughout the island and free medical attention and medication are provided for children and the aged. Prescriptions and drugs are available at the hospital and at pharmacies down-town. Visitors requiring special medication, however, are advised to travel with it.

Education

The education system reflects strong British influence. Pre-primary education is provided in nursery schools for three to five year olds; primary education for children between the ages of seven and eleven is provided in fifteen primary schools with infant, primary and post-primary departments. The post-primary departments are being grouped and re-organised in junior secondary schools, and there is one secondary grammar school. School leaving examinations, set by London and Cambridge syndicates, are still taken. Montserrat, however, is fully committed to the regional Caribbean Examinations Council and has already started to write its examinations. Montserrat has a technical school/college. University education is provided mainly by the University of the West Indies. The University's local Extra-Mural Centre is the island's chief agent of adult education.

Welcome

If you are looking for noise and neon, Montserrat is hardly your dream world. But simple pleasures, quiet beauty and people who are friendly and simple, without being naive, are all here, far from the madding crowd.

The tranquillity of Woodlands Beach

CHAPTER SIX
On Bush and Tree

Things Bright and Beautiful

The flora of Montserrat is typical of the West Indies, but it contains plants which were either accidentally introduced or were once cultivated and have now become weeds. Indigo is an example of the latter. Many orchids once bloomed below the 1500 feet level, but the numbers have been considerably reduced by careless cleaning and the need for firewood. A few species still brighten the day and perfume the night. Among these are the yellow *Oncidium urophyllum* which grows on cacti and even on stones, and the sweetly scented *Brassavola tuberculata* with its large white flowers. Both of these have become rare.

The upper slopes of mountains are thick with a wild palm dubbed 'mountain cabbage'. At the lower levels, down to about 1000 feet, fern groves abound and are perhaps the most beautiful form of vegetation on the island.

Various forms of cacti are present, especially on low level forests. The Turk's Cap cactus once flourished, but is now almost extinct. In 1930, a writer on Montserrat observed that two or three chops with a cutlass at one of these can bring to an end perhaps 50, or even 100 years of growth.

Montserrat has its liberal share of tropical fruits, all in their season. Mangoes bear profusely between May and August, many falling to waste in roads and ravines. Citrus, pineapples, avocado pears, sugar apples, mammie apple (locally known as man-support), soursops, guavas, strawberries, passion fruit, honeysuckle, melons, cashew, pawpaws and breadfruit abound.

The mango has just been selected as Montserrat's national tree, while the *Heliconia caribaea*, locally known as the lobster claw, was named the national flower.

When green, the pawpaw is cooked and eaten as a vegetable. In the late nineteenth and early twentieth century, papain from the pawpaw 'milk' was exported. The breadfruit, introduced from the South Sea Islands to the West Indies by Captain Bligh, is here in abundance. Originally food for slaves, the breadfruit is now prepared in a number of sophisticated forms and might easily be substituted for the Irish potato. It is served in cooked slices, mashed, in salad form, or even as chips. It may also be baked or roasted and eaten in lieu of bread.

Around 1928, bay trees occupied some 400 acres of land and bay oil distilled from the leaves was produced. Bay oil, also called bay rum, is a medicinal liquor used as a balm and a massage; it has similar properties to limacol and alcolado.

Dr Richard Howard, a distinguished United States botanist, who, in 1950, traced the chronology of botanic visits to Montserrat, lamented the paucity of collections and the 'lack of a general treatise on the plants'. A H R Briseback, a German botanist, gives forty-eight species of plants from Montserrat in his *Flora of the West Indies 1859-64*; John Ryan, a medical doctor who visited during the second half of the eighteenth century, sent his collections to

Wild heliconia — Heliconia caribaea

Copenhagen, where fifty-seven of them were described. Fifty-two were new to science, and three genera of flowering plants were based on Ryan's collections.

Dr Howard, who still visits the island out of botanic interest, was particularly interested in a black apple tree located in the Salem area, and collected by two previous botanists. Like the papaya plant, both male and female flower do not grow on the same tree. In Howard's view, the male flower has never been seen by a botanist. It would appear that Montserrat still offers a rewarding field of investigation for botanists.

Wildlife

Montserrat's wild animal population has been rightly described as modest in variety. Agoutis, birds, frogs, reptiles and a few species of fresh water fish complete the roll. A recent writer on the subject has noted, however, 'the naturalist and casual observer should still find Montserrat's animal life satisfying for the beauty, unusual appearance, and rarity represented in their numbers'.

The agouti, a game prize for dogs especially trained to sniff it out, is exquisite eating. Very few survived the chase and these, not without reason, steer clear of human haunts. They love the mountain, but a lowlander is occasionally seen hard by a thicket.

Bats, of which there are several species, complete the short list of native mammals. The fruit bat, a large nocturnal feeder, is said to be now very rare.

It is felt that the smallness of Montserrat and its distance from continents account for the paucity of animal life.

Some eleven species of reptiles have been identified, of which lizards are the most common. The green lizard, or anole, is seen everywhere on trees and around houses; the wood slave, or gecko, is frequently seen in or around the house at nights. Both are harmless and are considered useful in keeping the insect population in check.

The iguana is both beautiful and ferocious. Much

An iguana on the beach (Michael Bourne)

bigger than the 'house' lizard, it can be over four feet in length. It is coloured green, brown, grey and gold, in varying proportions. Sometimes, one of these colours is predominant. It is more frequently seen near the coasts, but it also inhabits mountains. The eggs and flesh of iguana are eaten, but they are not common articles of Montserratian diet.

The two species of snakes on Montserrat are both harmless. The black snake grows to a length of three feet and feeds on insects, lizards and rodents. The blind tropical worm snake, locally named the coffin borer, lives underground and is rarely seen.

Three species of 'frogs' comprise the island's amphibious family. They are the marine toad or crapaud, the tree frog and the 'mountain chicken'. The crapaud, reputedly the largest toad in the world, is essentially a nocturnal creature and inhabits lowland areas. As it crosses roads at night in search of insects, it sometimes falls victim to the traffic. Unlike the mountain chicken, it is not good for food, being 'ugly and venomous' as Shakespeare describes it.

In contrast to the crapaud, the tree frog is considered one of the world's smallest frogs. It is different too, in that it does not go through a live tadpole stage. Eggs are laid under a stone or log to hatch into miniature adults. The loud chirp of the tree frog has been described locally as 'an integral part of Montserrat's symphony of night noises'.

The mountain chicken, found only in Dominica and Montserrat, is regarded in both islands as a dining delicacy. This terrestrial frog can grow to a length of ten inches; it is hunted at nights on mountain slopes, its natural habitat. It is a threatened species which could soon disappear unless speedy conservation measures are taken.

If you see a flight of large white birds near the capital, it is not a Roman-type omen. These are cattle

MONTSERRAT ORIOLE Icterus oberi

25
cents

MONTSERRAT

A postage stamp depicting the Montserrat oriole — Icterus oberi *(Montserrat Philatelic Bureau)*

egrets going home to roost in a spectacular aerial display against the gold of sunset. Of some thirty land species of birds which breed on Montserrat, the egret is perhaps the most common. Hundreds fly daily to the island's fields and pastures where they feed on insects disturbed by grazing cattle or turned up by hoe and plough. At sunset, they wing their way to the Fox's Bay Bird Sanctuary, where they roost in trees in a mangrove swamp.

The bird sanctuary is also the home of several species of heron, coots, gallinules, cuckoos, king fishers and other water fowls.

The bird population includes the Montserrat oriole, found nowhere else in the world. It has been named the national bird. The oriole (*Icterus oberi*), a black and yellow bird with occasional splashes of gold in its plumage, is a beautiful sight in the mountains. It was first found at the head of the valley between Chance's and Farrell's peaks.

Doves, pigeons, thrashers, flycatchers and colourful humming birds are common. At least three species of humming birds are known. The two larger ones are mostly green with curved beaks, with one having a crimson throat. The third, which is the most common species, is smaller and has a straight beak and an emerald crest.

The killy hawk or kestrel, is the only resident bird of prey, although the red tail hawk, merlin and the peregrine falcon visit occasionally. Other birds include the frigate bird, which glides high in the air, and the brown booby, brown pelican, tropic birds, and terns which ply along the shore.

CHAPTER SEVEN
Customs and Culture

Some of the social and cultural customs and activities outlined in this chapter are dead or dying, but they nevertheless form an important part of the social history of the island. A number of social and cultural activities are connected with holidays and special seasons, the most important of which are St Patrick's Day, Easter and Christmas.

St Patrick's Day

In the eighteenth century, St Patrick's Day, March 17, was celebrated with feasts and festivities by the island's Irish inhabitants. In 1971, local scholars rediscovered the day, but saw it as a national day on which to celebrate the freedom fighters of the abortive 1768 slave uprising. Activities were based at the University Centre and took the form of cultural expressions — local plays, poems, folk singing, crafts and cuisine. A St Patrick's Day lecture on a topic of national importance is now delivered at the University Centre.

The St Patrick's Roman Catholic Church of Plymouth still holds an annual fund-raising dinner; St Patrick's village celebrates the feast over several days. The activities usually include a concert, dance and display of local dishes. Stable celebrations are still to

Carnival time

evolve, but there is a real danger that commercial activities might strangle the cultural and nationalistic aspects on which the 1971 rediscoverers of St Patrick's Day focussed.

Easter Time

On the Easter weekend, the winter garments of Lenten repentance are flung into the fires of song, dance, picnics, sea-bathing, excursions and Sunday School treats. The simpler pleasures of Eastertide, like the *vooming* of tops, the flying of kites, and children and adults skipping to the wheel of giant creeper-strings, are vanishing. So too is the custom of treating the white of an egg as a fortune telling oracle on Good Friday. The white of an egg put in a glass of water around midday took on shapes which indicated something of the fortune of the performer of the rite. If the formation resembled a bridal dress, marriage was betokened; if it looked like a gallows, death by hanging would result. Folks did not wash and iron on Good Friday, for when the neighbour's wife did it once, she bled through her nose, dyeing the clothes. Bonny-clabber trees were also 'known' to bleed on Good Friday.

It is on Easter Monday that the legendary mermaid of Chances Pond seeks contact with the inhabitants below. The mermaid guards a treasure chest at the bottom of the pond. To obtain the treasure, someone has to take the mermaid's comb on Easter Monday, run to the sea and wash it before being touched by a diamond snake which guards the mermaid and the comb. The victor will be rich forever. Although folks have seen the mermaid combing her long black hair, or think they have seen her, no one has been able to snatch the comb. So the treasure still lies at the bottom of Chances Pond!

August Monday

August 1 is Emancipation Day, and August Monday a national holiday, connected thereto. The celebrations take the form of picnic, bazaar and dance, and there is now little reference to the pristine jubilation of August 1, 1833. But freedom from peonage was once hymned and danced on village greens and unpaved streets.

> *Emancipation day done pass*
> *All buckra gonna nyam cut grass.*
>
> *Firs' o' August come agen*
> *Hurrah for Nincom Riley*
> *Buckra hit me, me hit him back*
> *Hurrah for Nincom Riley.*

This was a popular catch, Nincom Riley being the literate slave who read the emancipation proclamation for his fellows. A Long Ground man, born in August and called 'August' is famous for popularising it. This song and related impromptu celebrations have almost died out. August died in 1980.

Christmas Celebrations

Christmas celebrations are a nine-day carnival-like extravaganza, lasting from Christmas Eve to January 1. Today, formal activities begin as early as December 12; although these take place during the afternoons and at night, productivity on jobs and in offices begins to decline as the Christmas feeling infects the air. Christmas activities are now organised by a Festival Committee. The scheduling of events enables the hundreds of visitors as well as local persons to plan their entertainment programme and serves to ensure a broadening of and variety in the festive package. Something of the former spontaneity and folk nature of the celebrations is, however, lost.

Christmas Preludes
The braying of drums and the wacking of whips at village centres in November mean that masquerades are rehearsing. Children can gather round, for dancing mummers have not yet donned their frightening masks. Christmas is around the corner. Preliminary sounds, such as the following are receding:

> *Goodnight to the master and mistress of this house. We have come to remind you that Christmas is just fourteen days off. We wish you health; we wish you strength; we wish heaven's glory after death. What more can we wish you?*

These are the words of the spokesperson for a

serenading group, punctuating the singing of carols. They will return on Christmas Eve to remind you that 'Christmas is just around the corner'. You can then give them food, drink or money, as you wish. But this has changed within the last two decades. Householders now receive a notice of the visit, especially if they are middle class or expatriate. It is now essentially a fund raising effort mounted by churches and other community groups for some usually worthy cause.

On the Sunday evening before Christmas week begins, community singing groups gather at the town 'square' to sing carols and read the scriptures. This heralds the advent of the season.

Busy Week
Preparation for Christmas takes on a feverish pitch during the week before Christmas. Christmas foods are prepared: cassava bread made; yams and other root vegetables reaped, or *pragged*, to use the local patois; the sorrel, which fruits for Christmas, picked and made into a delicious non-alcoholic drink; cakes and plate tarts are baked; and pigs are killed on the eve of Christmas Eve, for Christmas is not Christmas without pork.

Christmas Eve
Some are busy with last minute shopping in the Plymouth stores; modern brass bands are blasting the air with music. But in quiet corners of villages, a 'jumbie table' is being set. This well decorated table, lavishly furnished with food — cassava bread, cakes, corn meal, meats and drinks — is a spread for dead ancestors, who are invited to partake in the Christmas feasting. They eat while the living inmates attend church. Thus, there is a meeting point between Montserrat folk religion and Christian religion. A

Donkey bath at Little Bay

jumbie is the spirit of a deceased person, who occasionally adopts a visible form and may sometimes take possession of a living person. The jumbie may come either for benign or malevolent purposes.

Village Days

St John's is a village in the Parish of St Peter. December 27, the feast of St John, is a day of special Christmas celebrations by the villagers. After morning worship in the Anglican Church, street dancing, feasting and revelry become the order of the day as Montserratians from every village descend on St John's adding to the fun and frolic. All the popular Christmas mummers used to be there: the Bull, masked, dressed in sackcloth and wearing horns sprouting from a hideous head dress, carries a two-pronged fork stick, the devil's sceptre, for he is both animal and the Devil; the Moko Jumbie, a costumed character made larger than life, performs on stilts; the Guppy, usually a female dressed in a brightly coloured housecoat (duster), her face profusely rouged and powdered, disguising the real features, is willing to reveal hotly coloured underwear; Miss Goosey, a very tall wooden puppet, is manipulated by a masked person on foot.

Many of these mummers have disappeared, queen contests and calypso shows taking their place. The gaiety and pageantry are still present, but the tone and ambience have changed.

Jealous of St John's Day, other villages have recently claimed festive days, although without any venerable basis. Christmas activities have thus become decentralised, with an Eastern Day and a Salem Day. Eastern Day activities are sited at Hyde Park, but they embrace the villages stretching from Long Ground in the far east to Lees. Masquerades, talent shows, queen contests and folk pageants feature in these village celebrations.

Beauty Contest

The first national beauty contest, or queen show, was organised by the Montserrat Junior Chamber (Jaycees) in 1965. Since then, it has become an integral part of the Christmas programme. Some five girls vie for the coveted title of island queen, a trip abroad and a shower of gifts. A creative element — singing, dancing, miming or monologue — is now a part of the competition.

Calypso Contest

This is as popular as the beauty contest. Eliminations take place before Christmas and are well attended. But on calypso final night, people stream into Sturge

Park like thirsty cattle, to listen to social comment in tempo and lyric. It is a communal affair; people argue and wager, and they quarrel when their imagined king is not the pick of the judges.

Alphonso Cassell (The Mighty Arrow), Montserrat's leading calypsonian, is an engaging performer. Calypso king for many years, he is now an international artist with a large following. The poet, musician and choreographer find consummate expression on an Arrow stage.

Costume Bands

A day in Christmas week, usually Boxing Day, is devoted to a contest and parade of costumed bands depicting historical events or scenes from contemporary life. The troupes are judged for colour, creativity, message, content, and presentation. The park becomes a carnival riot of colour and pageantry. The day ends with a street jump-up.

Drama, Song and Band Music

The new departure from traditional Christmas activities includes the programming of drama and choral music. The relevant groups, normally active throughout the year, prepare special presentations for the Christmas season. The leading cultural groups are the Montserrat Theatre Group, or groups derived from it; the Emerald Community Singers, founded in 1971, the Bethel Seventh Day Adventist Choir and the Montserrat Dance Theatre.

The String Band combines European and African instruments to produce unique indigenous music for dances, and other social occasions. It comprises a guitar, the Hawaiian ukelele (adopted), a triangle giving a tingling sound, the boom pipe, perhaps so-called from the sound emitted from blowing into this long pipe, a fife, and a shak-shak. The cast is made from tin or the calabash gourd which when filled with beads and shaken gives a sound not unlike the sound of the word, shak-shak. This harmonious ensemble plays modern songs, but serves traditional songs even better.

Night clubs come fully alive during Christmas. Brass and string ensembles with significant names like Hammah and Sledge, pound the night with rhythm as unwearied dancers tread an intimate measure.

New Year's Day

January 1 is greeted by the tooting of horns, the tinkling of glasses and the ringing of church bells. Some people begin the year in church; others at fêtes and dances. At daybreak, say 6.00 am, people begin to jump in the streets of Plymouth; it is the Christmas *jouvert*.

As the day wears on, Montserratians from every rural nook and cranny file into the town for the final fling. As late as the 1940's, that was the only day in the year when some folks came to town. Masquerades dance in the street; in the afternoon, the costumed bands of the 'Boxing Day' show parade the streets to the beat of music; the beauty 'queens' smile and royally wave, not from horse-drawn carriages, but from lumbering lorries. Then the final jump begins: life freezes to watch a seemingly endless technicolour of bobbing heads, prancing feet and girating backsides. This is called jamming; it is a packed procession; it is orderly confusion as

> *Rich prance with poor*
> *In annual rites to expiate*
> *Tomorrow's crimes of injured brotherhood.*
> *(Fergus)*

Masquerades

There is something unique about Montserrat masquerades, although there are marked resemblances to masquerades in other islands and even to the Jamaican and Belizean *Jonkonnu*. Masquerades are masked dancers (mummers) in colourful costume complete with bells, ribbons, small mirrors and an attractive tall head dress. They crack 'hunters' or cart whips to make way for themselves, to discipline each other, and, it is alleged, to ward off evil spirits. A troupe contains between six to nine dancers. It has a captain, usually identifiable by a ring in the nose of the mask. In addition to the first mate, who is second in command, there is a mischief, the smallest boy in the troupe and a queen, dressed in a duster, even though it is a male. Music is provided by a fife, a boom drum, a kittle drum, a shak-shak and a boom pipe.

Masqueraders and musicians

The kittle drum is a small goat-skin drum played with two sticks to give a syncopated rhythm; the boom drum is a bigger version played with one stick with a cushioned head to give the basic beat in a deep 'boom' sound. The shak-shak is a maracas, and the boom pipe is a length of ordinary pipe, which when blown into, gives out a 'boom' sound. The dances resemble warfare as well as religious ritual.

Masquerading is rooted in African folk religion. Some of the dance steps are westernised, but the syncopated drum beats are African. They dance quadrilles and polkas to the music of popular folk songs. Like wandering minstrels, they go from door to door and from village to village receiving gifts of drink and money. The precise meaning of the ceremonial costume of the masquerade is unknown, but a study of similar 'masques' and rituals in Africa suggest symbols of war, guardianship and fertility.

Masquerading, once an adult art, now involves children and at least one school, the Cork Hill Primary, has a troupe which performs across the island and overseas.

Masquerades now dance for the gaze of tourists at odd times in the year but, traditionally, the dance is a Christmas ritual. Masquerades constitute the richest folk ensemble in Montserrat. In 1973, they performed to wide acclaim at the first Caribbean Festival of Arts (CARIFESTA) in Guyana and at later festivals in Cuba (1979) and Barbados (1981). The masquerade is a folk art in its own right.

Jumbie Dance

The jumbie dance is the highest expression of folk religion in Montserrat. This is a religious-therapeutic dance as well as a dance to induce divination. The band, called a woo-woo band, consists of fife, triangle and a woo-woo or bobla drum which still exists in parts of Africa. This drum, which gives its name to the band, is made with a smooth taut goat skin which when rubbed with the hand produces an eerie 'woo-woo' sound. The sound helps to create the atmosphere for spirit possession and for subjecting jumbies to the will of men. It also sets the stage for African-like tribal dances which lead to the trance-like state, bringing into communion the worlds of the living and the dead for the good of the living. Cures and prognostications are then possible.

The dance is preceded by a lavish feast for the living, and the dead. A table is set in the middle of the house with meats, cakes and a large variety of drinks. Replete with food and liquor, the dancers progress from a slow waltz to quick quadrilles. The rhythm gets hotter and bare feet beat the wooden floor faster and faster until one or two dancers get possessed and begin to divine. Dancing could last all night spilling over into the next day. The 'spirit' may suggest a remedy (herbal, perhaps) or a new name (his or her name) for a sick child. Thus, kinship ties are closely associated with religious dance. Most times, it is a dead ancestor whose aid is evoked. The jumbie dance is disappearing and with it a rich matrix of folk culture and religion. There is some conflict, however, between those who regard the jumbie dance as a valid folk-religion and therefore a crucial aspect of the island's cultural identity on the one hand, and those who see it as an unchristian relic of the dark African past, unworthy of Montserrat in the last quarter of the twentieth century, on the other hand. Brass bands, steel bands, reggae and rock may well combine with western religion to obliterate this rich strand of the culture.

Jumbie music and jumbie lore will not go so easily, however, 'into that good night'. The music is played at rum shops or in homes where persons may oblige with quadrille dancing. It is even staged as an art form. In these instances, the sensation and supernatural are absent. One of the best known Montserrat artistes, Sam Aymer (alias Black Sam), now deceased, was a great fifer and an exponent of jumbie dance music. He played both for the jumbie ritual as well as for secular entertainment.

> *Black Sam, illiterate man?*
> *blowing yuh mind in concertos*
> *writing yuh name in sound*
> *piping yuh fame in the pain of history.*
>
> *Black Sam, black fife, black drum*
> *De jumbies' laureate.*
>
> (Fergus)

People still pay respects to, or demonstrate fear of, the dead: 'Beg pardon, I don't call yuh name for no harm', is heard if per chance the name of a deceased features in a conversation. Or the name of the dead is prefixed by the phrase, 'poor soul . . .' A bottle of liquor has to be 'broken' at the foundation of a house and sometimes when the roof is 'raised'; the first drops of a new bottle of liquor are poured on to the floor or ground for the dead to partake of.

Burial

As in most cultures, vital life events like christening and death receive special attention. In Montserrat, a *wake* is held at the home of the deceased on the night before burial day. The dead person is laid out on his or her bed (West Indian historian, Edward Brathwaite points out that in West Africa they were laid out in state) and kinsfolks, neighbours and friends gather in an adjoining room to eat and drink and sing funeral songs. Bread, salt fish, cocoa 'tea', coffee 'tea' and rum are the staple fare at wakes. The songs register a belief in the immortality of the soul.

In villages, most people except the sick, the aged, and the children, 'follow' the dead in a rather elaborate procession to the graveyard where unashamed and unrestrained communal weeping is not uncommon. The third night is rising night. Villages shut up early, but some of the daring see, or fancy they see, when the dead returns; and inmates of the house 'know' when the spirit of the deceased enters. Those who sleep with relatives of the deceased must continue to do so for at least nine days. On the ninth day, all the rites are over with the washing of the clothes of the deceased in the sea or river.

The wake in its pristine form is dying. In fact, with the provision of proper mortuary facilities at the public Glendon Hospital, it could totally disappear.

House moving

Maroons

In Montserrat, a maroon is not a runaway slave. It was a strategy — a communal approach to solving some of the problems of rural living. Friends and neighbours came together, some voluntarily, to help each other in certain tasks such as moving or building a house, cultivating the soil or harvesting a big crop.

At a maroon, food is provided in abundance. The menu usually includes the ubiquitous goat-water or saltfish and dumplings. To the extent that the Montserrat maroon denotes a style of community living alien to the normal run of middle and upper class society, it relates to the regular concept of maroon as an assertion of freedom and escape from societal regimentation.

Another communistic activity is the giving by some more successful person to a less fortunate, reliable neighbour, one or more head of stock to rear for which a half of the offspring (popularly referred to as 'the improvement') will be given in payment. There are no legal transactions; only a friendly, mutual agreement. These African-based communistic practices, like so many others, are dying. Ironically, the attempts to impose co-operatives officially have hardly been successful.

Penny Concert

Like much else, these concerts have almost vanished under the impact of modernisation. They were a regular part of village life sharing some of the principles of the maroon. The village came together to raise church funds through a variety concert mounted now by this brother, now by that sister, at a strategic spot in the village, usually in the open. The programme was unrehearsed, each item being offered at the beginning of the concert or while it is in progress. After each item of song, poem or 'speech', the crowd streamed forward to bang their pennies on the chairman's table in appreciation and applause. The relatives of the performer led the plaudit, often with the phrase, 'our side', a reference to kinship bond and the obligation to support the family name and achievements.

With a lively tongue, often lubricated by liquor, the chairman kept the concert alive, soliciting and garnering the collections, making snippets of oratory such as:

> The name of Napoleon Buonaparte shall die
> out
> The name of the Duke of Wellington shall
> die
> But my name, my pugnacious name shall
> never die.

In these concerts, the sacred and secular merged.

Speechifying was a regular feature at concerts. A speech was a hodge-podge of verses of songs (some adapted), and improvised poetry said with a racy rhythm; some statements had bits of Latin curiously linked with English; some phrases were nonsense phrases laced with appealing rhythm spoken to astound the hearers and evoke their praise. Here are some examples:

> Hail to the Lord anointed
> Great David greater son
> He came in the time appointed
> His reign on earth begun
> He came to break oppression
> To set the captive free
> To take away my boastingness
> And roll it in the sea.

As I was in yonder corner, I heard my most noble chairman call my name. As I look around and see so many charming ladies, it charms my heart to say a word or two out of my rignum signum dignum.

Chairman: *Ladies and gentlemen, time tempus fugit.*

Throughout a speech, there is constant audience participation as the speaker inquires: 'Mister Chairman, can I proceed?' If the audience approves, there is a chorus of response: 'Proceed until morning.'

Nicknames

Most Montserratians have two names, one for home — a 'pet' name, and another for school and church — an official name. The two names do not necessarily resemble each other, like Jim and James, and there is no necessary connection between them. Some actual examples are: Belle and Mary, Belle and Theresa, Narna and Florence or Billy and Rupert. Sometimes, the house or 'pet' name is a 'jumbie' name given to appease some dead person or to honour a deceased relative. Sometimes, it's just like having two pairs of shoes, one for school and the other for Sunday school.

Many second names are just nicknames, often bestowed as a mark of affection. Some attribute this custom to Irish influence. In 1956, an English Methodist minister recorded a number of these nicknames and their significance. A number of these persons are still alive today. Mary M Sweeney, an organist at the Cavalla Hill Methodist Church, was called 'Dovie'; George Silcott of the same area was 'Dada'. Mr William Osborne of Rocklands was called

'Governor' by his mother, because he was the only son of a large family. Mr Jonathan Daley of Bethel, a leading Methodist local preacher, is called 'Maas Barlow', because he was born on a Sunday morning when a visiting minister named Barlow was conducting the service at Bethel; 'Rainy' was so called because he was born during a heavy rain-storm.

Some names reflect native wit and humour. A St Patrick's man was called 'Rope Neck', because he had a long scraggy neck; a Long Ground woman was called 'Mistress Miller', because she was very fond of corn and made a loud noise when eating it; 'Bus Pot' earned his name because he reported that De Goberment Depot rice swell so much dat ih bus de pot (pronounced *pat* in dialect).

Native Dishes

The mountain chicken, a long-limbed terrestrial frog which grows to a length of about ten inches, is a local speciality, fried dry or stewed. It has a more delicate taste than ordinary chicken, and is found only in Montserrat and Dominica. The Hideaway, a guest house in Rocklands, specialises in frog legs.

Goat water, referred to earlier, is regarded as the national dish. This long goat stew, probably of joint Irish and African origin, is a must at christenings, weddings, house warmings, and jumbie dances. Here is the recipe for goat water:

2 quarters goat or sheep
4 onions, cut up
Herbs and chible (local name for scallions and thyme)
¾ cup cooking oil
3 oz fresh marjoram

4 cloves garlic, minced
1 tablespoon whole cloves, crushed
1 tablespoon mace
2 tablespoons catsup
1 hot green pepper, whole
Salt and pepper

Cut the meat into 2 inch cubes, being sure to leave the bones in. Wash in salt water and place in a large saucepan. Cover with cold water, bring to the boil and simmer, covered, for 5 minutes. Skim, and continue simmering, covered, adding remaining ingredients; add boiling water as necessary. When meat is nearly tender, combine 2 cups of flour with enough cold water to make a smooth paste. Stir enough of this mixture into the stew to give the desired thickness, and add some browning for colour. Half cover the pot and continue simmering until meat is done. Add some whiskey or rum if desired. Serve in cups or bowls, very hot, with the bones.

It is available at some restaurants and hotels, but it is the older folks who best prepare the savoury pottage. For one thing, they cook it on a wood fire, and the smoke enhances the flavour.

Legend

While on the subject of water, the visitor should drink from the stream at Runaway Ghaut — if he or she wants to return, that is, for

If you drink from that burn
You will surely return.

CHAPTER EIGHT
Things to See and Do

Montserrat is free from hustle, but there is much to see, and varied interests are catered to. The history enthusiast, nature lovers, the scenery buff, the hiker and the picnic person will all find the island engaging.

Historical Sites

The history enthusiast as well as those with a passing interest in the significant sites of the island will find the information in this section of the chapter valuable. The sites detailed here begin at Trant's, the main entrepôt, follow the main road to Plymouth and then northwards, ending at Runaway Ghaut. Finally, the Galway's Plantation Ruins in the south of the island are introduced. Of course, to reach some sites, one has to turn off the main highway from time to time. Tours to these sites are arranged by hoteliers, travel agents, taxi drivers and the tourist board. Some are within walking distance of Plymouth and the hotels and can be reached by following a Route Map or through the courtesy of a friendly Montserratian.

Trant's Estate, adjoining Blackburne Airport, was the site of an Amerindian village. Artefacts in the form of pottery, beads, clay deities, mascots, stone pestles and flints are still found there. A rich collection of these is said to have been either sold or donated to the Heys Museum in New York. The flints are not indigenous. Found in neighbouring Antigua, they may have come through travel and trade. The evidence is not conclusive, but the site appears to be Arawak rather than Carib. The artefacts indicate that Arawaks lived a rather settled life there, growing cassava and corn, worshipping their gods and burying their dead.

Arawakan artefacts have also been found in Dagenham, but the area is too sprawling and ill-defined to specify a site. Further investigation is necessary.

The Bethel Centenary Church is the most imposing and architecturally attractive Methodist church building on the island. It was built to commemorate a

The Methodist Church at Bethel

hundred years of Methodist activity on the island. Earliest Methodist efforts started in Montserrat in 1793 when 'a small company of about twelve persons, who are under the influence of grace, are regularly met, in a private manner, once a week by one of our pious brethren of colour, capable of instructing them in the things of God'. The Bethel Church was one of the few church buildings on the island to withstand the fury of the 1928 hurricane. On the morrow of the storm, its majestic head remained peaked towards heaven, and still does.

The Church of St George perches near a ravine in Harris Village. The present building has replaced a previous one destroyed by an earthquake in 1843. This church has been particularly vulnerable to national disasters. The hurricanes of 1899, 1924 and 1928 all took their toll. In the last one, the chancel toppled and the organ was destroyed. The old graveyard is a valuable source of historical information.

Fort St George occupies a commanding view of Plymouth and its harbour from St George's Hill, which rises to nearly a thousand feet. It is perhaps the last fort built on Montserrat. The exact date is not known, though it may have been connected with the 1781-82 Anglo-French clash which ended with Rodney's victory at the battle of Les Saints, off Dominica. The fort magazine is now almost over-covered by shrubs and creepers, but a number of cannons are displayed at the summit of the hill.

St George's Hill was not only connected with military protection. It also featured in hurricane precaution. As a cautionary signal for the probable approach of a hurricane, a red flag was hoisted on a signal staff at St George's Hill fort by day, or a rocket was fired therefrom at night. If the storm was imminent, all church bells would ring for ten minutes.

Three guns would be fired successively from the Treasury, and two rockets fired from St George's Hill whether at day or night.

St George's Hill is reached by a motorable road which branches off the main road from Plymouth to Blackburne, at the village of Gages. It was one of the spots toured by Queen Elizabeth II of Britain when she visited the island in 1966.

The first **St Patrick's Roman Catholic Church** of Plymouth was begun in 1842 by a Father Henry McNiece and was completed about 1848. It had to be rebuilt twice however, once in 1900, after its destruction by the 1899 hurricane, and again in 1929 following the 1928 hurricane. It is one of the most magnificent structures in the town of Plymouth, and

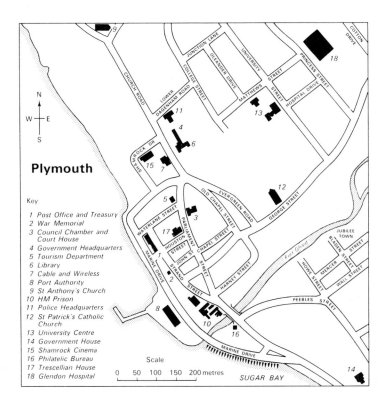

Plymouth

Key:

1 Post Office and Treasury
2 War Memorial
3 Council Chamber and
  Court House
4 Government Headquarters
5 Tourism Department
6 Library
7 Cable and Wireless
8 Port Authority
9 St Anthony's Church
10 HM Prison
11 Police Headquarters
12 St Patrick's Catholic
   Church
13 University Centre
14 Government House
15 Shamrock Cinema
16 Philatelic Bureau
17 Trescellian House
18 Glendon Hospital

Scale

0   50   100   150   200 metres

SUGAR BAY

it houses many interesting pieces of religious art.

It is suspected that the ruined Roman Catholic cemeteries at Streatham, O'Garro's and the former St Mary's School yard in Plymouth, were also sites of pre-1842 churches. If these churches existed, they very likely fell victims to anti-papal spoliation. Prior to the building of the St Patrick's Church, worship took place on the property named 'Trescellian House' (Shamrock House) now occupied by M S Osborne Limited. Located in upper George Street, its spires rise high and can be spotted from long distances around.

The Plymouth Gaol still bears its birth date, 1664. From 1640, Plymouth took over from Kinsale as the island's capital. A Protestant nucleus from England settled there, and it became the residence of most of the councillors. One reason for the choice of Plymouth was that it offered a superior anchorage to Kinsale Bay. Dagenham Beach may have been the centre of this second capital. The gaol sits in the heart of the town near the public market.

St Anthony's Church, the state church, is the most significant of all the church buildings. The original church was built in 1636 by the first Governor, Anthony Briskett 'for the Glory of God and Your Majesty's honour'. This Anglican church, in a Roman Catholic colony, has had a distinguished history and checkered fortunes. It has experienced ravages by earthquakes and hurricanes, demolition by Gallic invasions, and has variously been used as community centre, barracks for soldiers and a hurricane shelter, in addition to its central function as a place of solace for the soul.

Burned by the French when they invaded the island in 1666, and destroyed by an earthquake on Christmas day in 1672, it was rebuilt for the second time in 1673. Desecrated by the Caribs on their many raids, and finally demolished by the French on their

1712 invasion, it was rebuilt by Governor Stapleton on the order of Lord Willoughby in 1730. A stone near the vestry bears the inscription: 'Rebuilt in 1730'. The church was enlarged in 1895, only to be demolished four years later by the 1899 hurricane. Rebuilt in 1900, it became the victim of yet another hurricane in 1928.

Following a decision in 1930 to lower the floor of the nave, excavation revealed an early paving of ancient brick. Thus the transept is very likely a part of Briskett's 1636 church 'of stone and brick'.

The tablets on the walls of the church bear valuable records of Rectors and English families of the eighteenth and nineteenth centuries. One tablet reveals, for instance, that a Reverend J Collins was parish priest for twenty-three years. The church still holds two silver communion plates and two chalices, which were donated by the slaves as an offering of thanks to God for their emancipation. This was a touching act of piety, especially if, as tradition has it , slaves who accompanied their master to the church yard waited outside in obedience to the sign: 'No slaves or dogs allowed'.

The church has given the name Church Road to the last few hundred yards of Parliament Street, which ends at the church gate.

Sturge Park, a short walk north of the St Anthony's churchyard, and fringed on the west by the Caribbean Sea, has been for many years the national sporting park. The five-acre green was donated to the people of Montserrat in 1936 by the directors of the Sturge's Montserrat Company in memory of the founding father, Joseph Sturge, the English humanitarian and real estate speculator. The park is a leisurely stroll to the north of Plymouth. The pavilion provides a vantage spot from which to view games, but it also commands a panoramic sweep of great beauty ranging from sea to mountain.

Old Road Town, around Vue Pointe Hotel, is important as a place and a memory, even if there is nothing left to see, since it was probably the site of the very first European settlement. It was named from Old Road in St Kitts whence the first settlers came. A map of Montserrat, drawn in 1673 during the governorship of Colonel William Stapleton, names Old Road Bay as Brisket Bay. The town was then named **Stapleton Town**. Both Anthony Brisket and William Stapleton gave their names to their first townships. It was abandoned as a major town for healthier sites at Kinsale and Plymouth. In 1696, however, there was still a township there, because it was described together with Bransby and Carr's Bay as more 'remote and not so well inhabited as other parts of the island'. These settlements were still then considered worthy of a landing guard of at least four men. The little town was burnt by the French in 1712.

Runaway Ghaut of history and legend is a mile north of the village of Salem. In their invasion of 1712, the French, who had landed some of their soldiers at Carr's Bay, were burning their way south. At Runaway Ghaut, a Captain George Whyke engaged the French in a heroic battle. With a force of some sixty men, he held the ghaut long enough to allow the inhabitants in the region to make for the safety of the mountains. The French had landed 3,500 men but all were not thrown into the Runaway Ghaut battle. The ravine on the south side of the road, where Runaway Ghaut runs to the sea, is known as Frenchmen's Creek. The remnant of a cemetery at Carr's Bay may well contain the remains of the casualties of that war.

Galway's Plantation Ruins: The most valuable remnants of a Montserrat sugar plantation buildings are to be found on the road to Galway's Soufriere. An ambitious project, sponsored by the Montserrat National Trust, has been launched to study the ruins and identify the various buildings and sections of buildings. The architectural beauty of the well-crafted stone buildings have been brought into sharp focus. Typical plantation buildings like the Great House, the boiling house and the tower mill have already been identified, and valuable artefacts have been discovered. The ruins promise to be an extremely valuable archeological site. The declared ultimate aim of the project is to study the Galway plantation community. The first Galway's plantation was established in the seventeenth century and may have been owned by Irishman David Galway, a prominent Montserratian plantocrat of the time. A 114 page report on the project, *Galway's Plantation, Montserrat, West Indies*, has been published.

Beyond Galway's Soufriere and between it and the South Soufriere Hills, lies **The Garden**, a redoubt allegedly built in 1666 against the first French invasion. The third Governor of Montserrat, Anthony Briskett Jr, and two hundred English men were captured there by the French, with the help of Caribs. A small fort and old cannons are still there, although at the time of writing, the site stands in need of clearing.

Places of Interest

This section of the chapter locates and describes places of interest other than historical sites, although some overlapping is naturally to be expected. This time, we begin the tour in Plymouth and go north-ward to as far as Blake's, veering and inclining left and right as interests beckon. Returning to Plymouth, we go southward via Government House to as far as the Great Alp Falls.

The Public Library, which functions as the national library, is located on the ground floor of the main Government administration buildings on Church Road in Plymouth. It is open from 9.00 am to 4.30 pm daily from Monday to Saturday, except on Wednesdays when it is closed, and Saturdays when it is open from 9.00 am to 1.00 pm. There is always a cheerful and knowledgeable staff on hand to help. The library contains, among its valuable holdings, Stapleton's informative 1673 *Perimeter Map of Montserrat*, a copy of which he sent to the Lords of Trades. This, the earliest map of Montserrat, purports to record all plantations, towns and places of interest which existed then. It is evident from the map that only the coastal areas of the island were settled in 1673. The map contains a key to the names of people and places. It is included in the *Blathwayte Atlas* published by Brown University, Rhode Island, United States of America. It is an invaluable guide to the physical layout of seventeenth century Montserrat.

The Public Library also houses a number of socio-historical documents on Montserrat, not normally available elsewhere. These include unpublished theses, typescripts, and published articles.

A sugar mill tower on Richmond Hill is the home of the **Montserrat Museum**, which was set up by the Montserrat National Trust. The tower overlooks Sturge Park and St Anthony's Church and may be reached by turning left off the northern main road just beyond the Grove Botanic Station. The museum is open from 3.00 pm to 5.00 pm on Sundays, except during the tourist season (December to April), when it is also opened on Wednesdays from 1.00 pm to 5.00 pm. Entrance is free, but donations are accepted. The museum was opened in May 1976, and is largely the work of Montserrat's expatriate residents who came in the wake of the new real estate boom of the early

Montserrat Museum

1960's. The permanent holdings and archives of the museum keep growing and there are valuable artefacts and items on the socio-history of the island. Among the interesting holdings of the museum is a complete collection of Montserrat stamps. Periodic (and often topical), historical and cultural displays spark one's imagination and provide an educational experience. The museum structure, an eighteenth century sugar mill, is itself a historical piece.

On the beach at the foot of Springs Hotel, an exhilarating **Spa** bathes the weary and rheumatic. The water is pumped from a seventy-five foot deep well, via a picturesque stone fountain yellowing with sulphur, into a circular spa. The water, as in nearby **Hot Water Pond**, is sulphuretted; but here there is no haunting mystery, no spirit to placate with copper coins. Just step into the mineral flow and soak up energy and balm at every pore. Request for spa service should be lodged with the Springs Hotel. A cold water whirlpool adjacent to the spa makes this a unique bathing spot with the sea only two bodies' length away. A serpentine road, west of the museum, leads to the hotel and the spa; it can also be reached by a northward walk from Plymouth along the beach.

A left turn off the Grove Road just beyond the museum turn, takes one on to the Fox's Bay road; at the end of the road, near the beach, is the **Fox's Bay Bird Sanctuary**. Established in 1979 by the Montserrat National Trust, it is a haven for birds and a haunt for bird watchers and hikers. The sanctuary, 15 acres of swamp and soggy saline water, is fit only for the growth of mangrove and manchineel, but there is a central pond in which some of the birds swim. The beautiful cattle egret lives there and a number of other birds, including herons, cuckoos, kingfishers and the pied billed grebe. Snakes, lizards, iguanas and crabs also live in this animal reserve. Marked trails lead to the interior of the swamp.

Montserrat boasts one of the most modern recording studios in the world. Owned by Englishman, George Martin, **Montserrat Air Studios** sit on a hilltop at Waterworks, with a magnificent view of mountain, sea and valley. The 15 feet long control panel of the studio can receive, modulate, mix and record 46 separate tracks of sound. Commenting on the sophistication of the equipment, one visitor said he felt he had made a landfall into the twenty-second century. George Martin is said to have recorded all but one of the albums of the Beatles — not in Montserrat. Only top international stars of the stature of the Beatles, however, make use of the Montserrat facility. Limited accommodation is available in the adjoining mansion. Montserrat Air Studios are about 10 minutes' drive northward from Plymouth with a right turn at Belham River. Tours of the studio are arranged by appointment (Tel. 5678).

The Blakes Road, which runs from the north of the island through to Trant's near Blackburne, provides a scenic repast for motorist and walkers, with awesome cliffs dropping sheer into the sea on the billowy northeast coast. The road derives its name from Blakes Estate which it borders. The ruins of the estate buildings may well yield useful artefacts to careful search. Blakes Estate has a long history associated with three brothers, Henry, John and Martin Blake of Galway in Ireland. They were living in Barbados until 1675 when Henry and John purchased an estate in Montserrat. Henry sold his share to John who made a fortune from Blakes Estate before he died in 1692. Some of his hybrid descendants carrying the name Blake still live in the area near the beginning of the Blakes Road. The road project is jointly funded by the British Government and the European Development Fund.

From rising ground above Wapping Village, **Government House**, the official residence of the Queen's representative, keeps a watchful eye on Plymouth harbour. The pleasant Victorian mansion, built mostly of wood, is open to visitors on Wednesdays from 10.00 am to 12.00 am and the gardens on all week days, 10.00 am to 12.00 am. The gardens are well-kept with a good variety of ornamental plants. The house contains a small but interesting collection of paintings, artefacts, pieces of antique furniture, and souvenir crests from visiting warships. The house also holds some of the island's archives. The Governor's office, which is the seat of the Executive Council, is situated in one of the rooms.

Galway's Soufriere looks with misty brow over the southwest corner of the island. Rising some sixteen hundred feet, it is one of the several volcanic craters in the southern area of the island. The Galway's crater covers a fairly wide area, as vents and fumaroles keep shifting positions. The bubbling, boiling crater emits greyish-yellow molten sulphur and other chemicals. (The heat from the boiling puddles would be ample to cook an egg.) As one approaches the Soufriere, a strong smell of sulphur hits the nostrils. The smell is sometimes not dissimilar to that of a rotten egg! One can hike up White River bed to the Soufriere, but it is more usual to drive by a paved road which turns off the St Patrick's/O'Garro's Road into Galway's.

Great Alp Falls, south of the Soufriere, is in the same neighbourhood, but to get there, one must drive further along the O'Garro's Road, and then hike up river and mountain-trail for about an hour. The scenery en route has its own reward, but the final prize is a seventy-foot cascade. Plunge under, and savour it; the water is sweet to taste, and invigorating on the body.

Radio Antilles, sometimes called Big A or the Spirit of the Caribbean, is apparently the largest and most powerful commercial radio station in the Western Hemisphere. With a power output of 200,000 watts

Great Alps Falls

from its main transmitter and a coverage of some 800,000 square miles, it is hard to beat. In the day-time, it beams from the Virgin Islands in the north to Guyana in the south. At night, when the signal strengthens, it speaks to Puerto Rico, Cuba, Jamaica, Columbia, Venezuela and Surinam. Radio Antilles is famous for its comprehensive regional and worldwide newscast at 6.00 pm. It has also grown to be a power-fully informative and educational station. When it calls itself the Caribbean Information Centre, it is not a hollow boast. Broadcasts go out in English, French, and German. Most bus and car tours make Radio Antilles their southmost terminal point. In-house tours and demonstrations are courteously given. To illustrate the power of the station, attendants hold up a fluorescence tube near the live transmitting line. The tube immediately bursts into light. The Antilles Radio Corporation, to give it its formal name, was formed on April 20, 1963, with a registered office in Plymouth. Ownership of the station, which operates on both short and medium wave, is based in Germany.

Recreation and Amusement

Sports

Cricket, a national sport, is played between February and July, when a number of local teams compete in an organised league, on Saturdays and Sundays. The league culminates in a Leeward Island tournament at which an island XI represents the country.

Football or soccer is played in the latter half of the year. Once a crowd-drawing national sport played at a high standard, the level of soccer playing has declined as well as the numbers of spectators.

One of the newest and fastest growing sports is

Basketball, played on a Plymouth court. It has out-distanced all the other sports in its drawing of large enthusiastic crowds.

A **Netball** League Competition, which runs from April to July, has always been very popular. Teams from all over the island compete in the league bringing their supporters with them. Netball and basketball share court, league, and fanatic followers, with matches usually staged on the same nights. Games are played near the Shamrock Cinema in Plymouth.

Tennis, played on paved courts, was once a sport of the Montserrat well-to-do. Today, players come from all ranks of the society. Courts exist at the Vue Pointe (flood-lit) and Springs Hotels, and more are envisaged in the new fun and sports park to be built in Dagenham.

Volley-ball is played on a court near the YWCA building in Dagenham.

Golf is available at the beautifully set Belham River Valley golf course which covers an area of near 100 acres. It has 11 holes so arranged that it can be played as two 9-hole courses with different tees for each nine. The island has a number of excellent golfers who acquit themselves well in regional tourneys. The Montserrat golf club is sometimes host to such tournaments.

A number of black sand beaches provide excellent **Swimming**. These include Wapping Beach near the Yacht Club, Emerald Isle Beach, near Springs Hotel, Fox's Bay, Isles Bay, adjoining the Golf Club, Old Road near Vue Pointe Hotel, Lime Kiln Bay, Woodlands Beach (with beach hut facilities) Bunkum Bay, Carr's Bay and Little Bay, the last three being in the far north of the island.

In contrast to the black sand beaches, Rendezvous Bay, in the far north, has a coral beach. This 'hidden' beach is reached by boat from Little Bay or Old Road Bay or by a mountain trail.

Yachting is best arranged through Vue Pointe Hotel and the Yacht Club at Wapping, just south of the town centre. The Club has facilities for 'sunfish' sailing. For **Snorkelling**, the Vue Pointe Hotel should be contacted, but its facilities are limited mainly to guests. A diving club is connected with the Yacht Club.

Racing was never a common Montserrat past-time although the occasional horse race, or a donkey derby on a holiday, is not unknown. **Crab Racing** has, however, caught the local fancy and is occasionally a special feature at some hotels. Winning or losing, it is fascinating.

Activities of Clubs and Organisations

Two international organisations, **Rotary** and **Jaycees**, are active on the island. Rotarians meet for breakfast every Thursday at the Defence Force Club in Plymouth. Visiting rotarians are welcome to these breakfasts. A guest speaker is often invited to address the Club on some topic of interest to them or of general community interest.

Jaycees, essentially a leadership training organisation for young citizens, sponsors a number of sporting and cultural projects. Among these is the all-island Queen contest in December. The Junior Jaycees, a new offshoot of the adult movement, organises an annual Caribbean Disco Dancing competition around April.

Trojans, a youth organisation, mounts an all-Caribbean Beauty Contest on the Saturday preceding Whit Monday.

Activities of Cultural Groups

Montserrat **Theatre** has grown both in quantity and quality between 1970 and the present time. Plays dealing mostly with Caribbean issues are staged intermittently throughout the year by various groups, some ephemeral, others rather more permanent. The focus of drama is the playhouse of the University Centre (Tel. 2344) in Dagenham.

There are usually at least two active **Dance Groups**, even if performances may be four months apart. Dance theatre, like regular drama, is mostly staged at the University Centre. Membership is fluid and temporary residents and even visitors are readily absorbed into dance groups.

The University Centre, the local adult education arm of the University of the West Indies, runs an ongoing Creative Writing Workshop every Monday at 7.30 pm. The Workshop sometimes stages public Poetry Readings.

The **Alliouagana Music Centre** at Fort Barrington teaches various types of instrumental music and mounts performances from time to time. The famous Montserrat choral group, the Emerald Community Singers, is closely associated with the Music Centre. It gives a Christmas and a mid-year concert and sings for many a public and community event. The group performs at the Vue Pointe Hotel between December and April.

Miscellaneous Entertainment

It is Montserrat's deliberate policy to avoid casinos and over-many night clubs. A number of night spots with interesting names are, however, available. These include 747 Discotheque on Harney Street, Barefoot Disco at Streatham, The Agouti at Wapping and

Maximus Night Club, south of Plymouth and Kinsale.

These fun spots swing only on certain nights and more especially on weekends and holidays. There is no formality, no bars, but liquor bars. It is easy to join the frolic, for here as in hotels, 'our house is your house'.

Steel band music is not nearly as common as it should be in Montserrat, the steel band being a Caribbean invention. On Wednesday nights, however, barbecue night at the Vue Pointe Hotel, steel band music is provided for dancing or just for listening pleasure.

During the tourist season, from December to April, hotels draw on the cultural and arts group to provide entertainment for guests and other clients. Steel band, dance, theatre, piano music and choral singing are among the entertainment offered.

Christmas time is the season of entertainment and merry-making *par excellence;* it is the time of 'carnival', when concerts, dances, fêtes, house parties, cultural and artistic shows crowd the calendar.

Cinema

Montserrat has but one cinema, the Shamrock Cinema, which shows films nightly with double features on weekends and a Children's Matinee on Saturdays at 1.00 pm. The cinema is also the venue of the occasional live show featuring Caribbean and International artistes.

Ceremonial Parades

A British colony, Montserrat has inherited some of the ceremonials of the motherland, even if they are not 'thrice-gorgeous' or near as colourful as the Trooping of the Colour at Whitehall. The sitting of the Supreme Court in early March, July and November, opens with a judge inspecting a guard of honour made up of members of the Royal Montserrat Police Force; a new Governor is greeted at his swearing in ceremony with a guard of honour and one pays the last honours at the airport at his end of tour.

The most colourful and engaging is the **Queen's Official Birthday Celebration** in early June at Sturge Park. Proceedings begin with the arrival of the Governor in ceremonial dress, plumes and all, escorted by an *aide-de-camp*. The guard of honour comprising the Montserrat Defence Force, The Royal Montserrat Police Force, the Secondary School Cadet Corps and a number of 'lesser breeds' march past and do precision drills to the sound of martial airs and music of empire. The Queen arrives symbolically' and, at her imagined presence, the royal standard is hoisted. There is a *feu de joie* from blank cartridges, the national anthem is played and the crowd departs entertained and inspired by its annual booster of imperial patriotism.

The **War Memorial** service in early November is more low-keyed, but also more solemn. It is really a multi-denominational service to honour the fallen of World Wars One and Two. Troops are drawn up, the Governor arrives, wreaths are laid, songs sung, the roll of the dead called, Laurence Binyon's *For the Fallen* is quoted and the last post sounded. Uniformed bodies march past the Governor and the pensive crowd breaks. Following the service, ex-servicemen (the living ones) are treated to drinks at Government House.

Tours and Hikes

Island motor tours, calling at many of the historic sites and places of interest described in this chapter, are readily arranged by hoteliers and Tourist Bureau officials. Typical tours go as far south as Radio Antilles at O'Garro's and as far north as Blakes. The new Blakes-Trant's Road makes for a longer round-the-island motor route.

Ample opportunities exist for hikers to get among the island's wooded hills and clamber up the mountains. Most mountain tops are accessible, and a number of trails have been established. One popular and interesting foot tour takes you south from Long Ground via Tar River and Ghaut Mefraimie through Roche's (the southernmost point of the island), and through the Bamboo Forest terminating at Galway's Soufriere. This route takes you through the heart of a number of estates which once emptied bales and bales of sea-island cotton on the English market. In addition to a variety of trees and wild flowers, you will see scattered vegetable gardens and charcoal burning by a centuries-old method.

During the tourist season, a hiking group explores a different locale every other Saturday. They meet either at the Public Library in Plymouth, or at Belham Bridge or Woodlands. Leadership changes, but a Bert Wheeler of Old Towne is a constant contact. Newcomers are always welcome. Enthusiasm in this group often taps the limits of endurance.

With Montserrat's relatively slow automobile traffic, there is scope for leisurely strolls. A walk along the harbour road in Plymouth is pleasant. Notice the graceful war memorial set in a small square grassed 'island' and one or two attractive colonial

The War Memorial in Plymouth

buildings nearby. At the end of the jetty which rides a semi-deep water harbour, one gets a good view of Plymouth and its environs. Watch the measured eastern rise, from housetop to sloping farmland, from farmland to hills, from hills to mountains including Mount Chance greying its head in the clouds.

Walks in the countryside hold a different kind of interest. The roads are paved with peace, but look for beautiful vistas and roads through trees spanning ravines. Stand on Fogarty's Hill and gaze towards Cudjoe Head for one such vista, or just stand and savour,

> the sizzling breeze on Forgathy's that whistles
> to the mountain dove
> his subtle notes of love.
> (J A G Irish, Montserratian Poet)

Nature lovers can of course go bird watching at the Fox's Bay Bird Sanctuary or search among the mountains for the oriole, a bird found only in Montserrat. If they are lucky enough to be on island then, they can join the Garden Tour organised by the Rotary Club. Some of these gardens are mini-botanical gardens with large varieties of plants.

Cruise

Opportunities exist for sea cruising in addition to sunfish sailing with the Yacht Club. The police 'coast guard' launch, the *Emerald Star*, has in the past arranged a sail on the Caribbean side of the island for visiting parties. They may be contacted at Police Headquarters in Plymouth. For yachting from Old Road Bay to Rendezvous, contact the Vue Pointe Hotel. Rendezvous is the northernmost bay on the island.

A longer cruise takes you to Redonda, the half

square mile, round, volcanic island 12 miles north of Montserrat. Ocanmanru, as the Caribs called Redonda, was mined for phosphates between 1865 and 1912. It was annexed by Antigua in 1872 and is now constitutionally part of the state of Antigua and Barbuda, its proximity to Montserrat notwithstanding. Redonda stamps were issued as recently as 1978 when a Post Office was installed there.

There is a Redonda legend connected with a prolific novelist and literary figure, M P Shiel, born in Montserrat on July 20, 1865. Shiel senior took charge of the island in 1865 and persuaded the Bishop of Antigua to crown his young son as king. The present monarch is T Jon L Wynne-Tyson of Sussex, England, whose reign began in 1970 and who is legally the Executor for the Estate of M P Shiel. In 1978, Reynold Morse, a researcher into Shiel's literary legacy and legend, organised an expedition to his fifedom, Redonda, taking along the reigning king. On Good Friday, April 13, 1979, at 11.35 am, the king waved his flag over the island, 'blue for the sea, brown for the rocks and soil, and green for the verdure of Redonda — all made from pairs of old royal pyjamas by Her Royal Highness, Jennifer Wynne-Tyson'. One hopes that seeds of another Falkland-type conflict were not sown to fruit in bitter war among future Antiguans and Redondans, and for that matter, Montserratians. Make your own landfall from Montserrat, and be king, for a day.

Shopping

Shopping in Montserrat has greatly improved in recent years, both in the variety and quality of the products, and in the availability of locally made souvenirs. Shops carry attractively designed pottery, china and glass. Mohair stoles from Scotland, enamelware from Norway, furniture from Denmark, hand-screened prints, woollens, and a variety of clothing are among the general shopper's choice.

Several Plymouth stores offer locally made souvenirs. The Government Craft Shop on Parliament Street sells hand-woven gift items made from local sea-island cotton, and leather goods made from locally tanned leather. Tapestries with hand-drawn designs and miscellaneous hand-crafted pieces can be bought at outlets in Plymouth; items of glass and ceramics are produced at a studio in Olveston; unique, local jewelleries are sold at the Unique Gift Shop on George Street. Paintings by local artists are put on the market from time to time; articles made from indigenous material, and generally reflecting the island's culture, are on the increase. The day when Montserrat souvenirs are made in Birmingham may not be over, but it is certainly on the wane.

Epilogue

A morning in Montserrat
after dark rain
is a poem in puberty
a half-spun refrain

water beads dance
prisming the light
shimmer on the eaves
like iridescent pearls

tittering birds
sip light from the sun
dew from the leaves
genuflecting their praise.

from *Stop the Carnival* by H A Fergus

Selected Reading*

DEWAR, A M   *Music in the Alliouagana* (Montserrat) *Cultural Tradition*, Unpublished Dissertation, University of the West Indies

DOBBIN, J D   'Religion and Cultural Identity — The Montserrat Case', *Caribbean Issues*, Vol. IV, No. 1, April 1980

ENGLISH, T S   *Ireland's Only Colony: Records of Montserrat* (Unpublished) 1930

FERGUS, H A   *History of Alliouagana: A Short History of Montserrat*, University Centre, Montserrat, 1975

FERGUS, H A   *Montserrat, the Last English Colony: Prospects for Independence*, University Centre, Montserrat, 1978

FERGUS, H A   'Montserrat Colony of Ireland: The Myth and the Reality', *Studies* (Dublin) Winter 1981

HALL, D   *Five of the Leewards*, Barbados, Caribbean University Press, 1975

IRISH, J A G   *Alliouagana in Focus*, Plymouth, Montserrat, 1973

IRISH, J A G   *Alliouagana in Agony: Notes on Montserrat Politics*, Plymouth, Montserrat, 1974

MESSENGER, J   'The Influence of the Irish in Montserrat', Caribbean Quarterly, Vol. 13, No. 2, June 1967

MESSENGER, J   'African Retentions in Montserrat', *African Arts*, Summer, 1973

MESSENGER, J   'The Most Distinctively Irish Settlement in the New World', Ethnicity 2, 1975

PHILPOTT, S   *West Indian Migration: The Montserrat Case*, London, Athlone Press, 1972

SOMERVILLE, D   *The Early Years of Montserrat: a Chronicle of the People Who Settled the Island*, (Unpublished Typescript) Plymouth, 1975

The Old People's Welfare Association   *The Montserrat Cook Book*, Plymouth, 1973

*The Montserrat Public Library may be consulted on this Reading Material.